Jennifer

Happy Birthday!
I hope you enjoy this
gift of love! Nadia ♥

Art & Inspiration
by Faith L. Hazell

Dedication

I dedicate this book
to all of you who have invested in a beautiful family in Africa.
A family full of love, children and laughter.
Your compassion has already made a difference.

I dedicate this book
to my husband
who helped me endlessly with my silly questions
and any and all the crazy computer stuff I had to do.

I dedicate this book
to my family
who got goose bumps when I told them what I was doing.
They ran with me, constantly encouraging the work I was doing.

I dedicate this book
to my friends and co-workers.
They let me dream,
spurred me on
and didn't get tired of the countless hours
I talked to them about the designs,
the book cover and the name.

Lastly, I dedicate this book
to the **Tumaini Children's Home** in Africa.
May you be blessed with enough;
enough joy,
enough money,
enough wonder
and more than enough love
for each and every one of you.

Foreword

When I began to design this line art colouring book, I had some physical issues with my heart. I had palpitations that plagued me. They were there almost constantly. I began to slow down my life in order to accommodate the fact that my heart would start beating too fast, my body would get extremely weak and ordinary tasks seemed monumental.

Simultaneously, a friend suggested I publish a book of my doodles and from that, this idea was born. Sitting down to create, became a safe place for me. It became a haven. It was a place to go away from the chaos, away from the incessant crazy beating of my heart and away from the debilitating fear surrounding it.

What became interesting to me is that as I was dealing with my physical heart, God began to do some work on my spiritual heart. Later in this book I have included a piece of writing that explains further what was happening in my physical heart as well as my spiritual heart.

As he began shaping, healing my heart I noticed that many of my doodles actually include hearts. As I wrote devotionals and chose devotionals from my blog and chose Scriptures, those also mirrored love. Without me realising it or orchestrating it whatsoever, this book seemed to be woven together with the message of love. As I began to see this, suddenly I was struck with another thought. How fitting it is that I am donating the proceeds of this book to a children's home in Africa!!!! This seemed to be a symbol of what God was doing in me. This book is not only my art - it is part of my heart.

As you work through this book, let the Creator of your heart, do some healing work. Gentle touches of his hand, will heal, inspire and encourage you into the next season of your life.

How to Use this Book:

Welcome to the world of line art. I am so excited that you are here.

I want you to make this book your own. You can colour it with pens, pencil crayons or water colours. You can add bling, or paper or scraps or your own line art. You can colour bits and pieces or fill in white spots that I purposefully left. Journal in it on the blank pages or in the borders. Or you can leave it black and white altogether as each page is a hand drawn piece of art work, meant for you to enjoy. We have intentionally put a border around each picture so that you don't lose any of the picture in the binding and each piece stands on its own. Make this book your own book and grace the pages with your personality.

There are a few things to be mindful of. I printed only on one side of the paper so that the colours would not interfere with a drawing on the other side. However, if you are using watercolour or markers, it would be a good idea to put card stock or cardboard under the page you are colouring on so that the colours don't bleed onto the next page.

I have included some book marks and cards in the back that you can enjoy. Please feel free to glue the book marks onto card stock so that they are sturdier when you are using them in a book.

My hope is that it relaxes you, inspires you, entertains you, and that you will love it as much as I do.

Have fun!

Faith Hazell

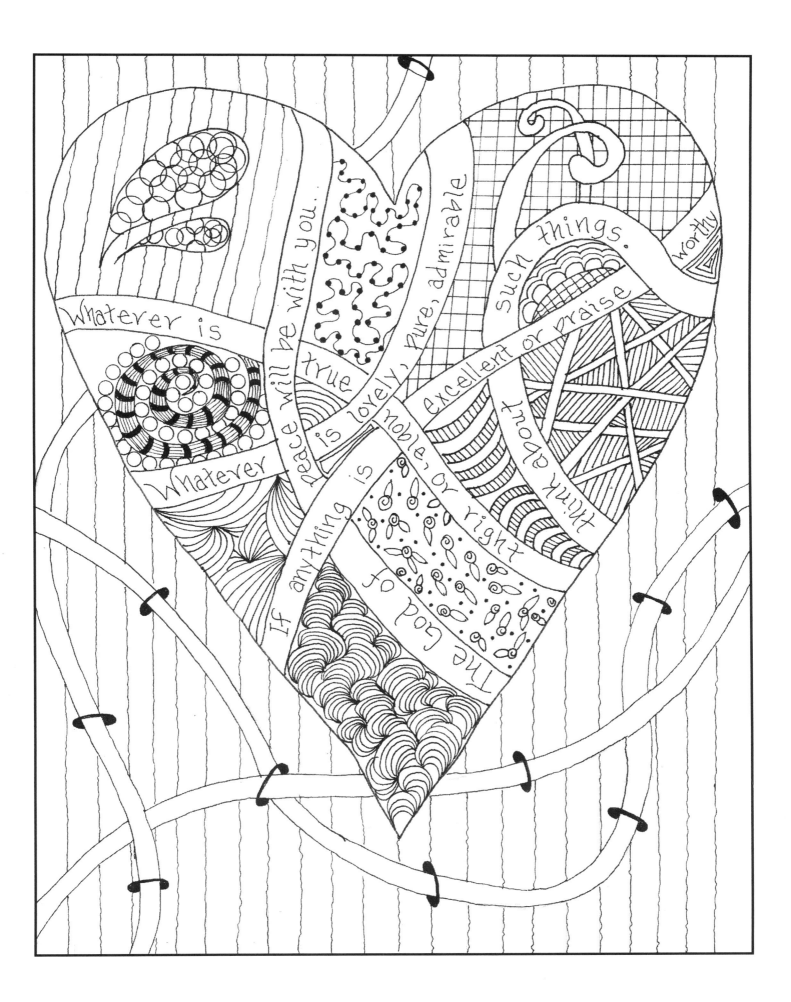

Have you tried turning it off and on again ?

Have you ever heard of the computer tech guy saying, "Have you tried turning it off and on again?" to a frantic customer who calls in about a computer not acting right?? There is even a show on the television whose signature is this very question because it's about some guys who are set in an office that fixes computers.

Apparently, the body works very similar to that. A few weeks ago, I had to have a procedure called a cardioversion. It is a procedure where an electrical current is sent to the heart to make it stop for only a second. Then they start it up again in hopes that it regains a correct rhythm - much like a computer. Because I am not actually a computer, but a HUMAN, I was terrified about it - imagining all kinds of scenarios. It does come with risks, but so does crossing the street every morning. I felt much better about it after talking to the doctor. He was able to calm my fears and put some perspective into the situation.

As one does when they are coming close to a day that they think might be significant I have done a lot of soul searching these last days. I wasn't sure what to expect. I have asked God to show me if there are things in my spiritual heart that does not resonate with the One who created me. I have searched my heart to make sure that it is soft and pure before God and people around me. It's interesting that many times a physical issue mirrors a spiritual issue. Jeremy and I have seen this many times.

David in the Bible said this: Search me, O God, and know my heart; Try me and know my anxious thoughts; And see if there be any hurtful way in me, And lead me in the everlasting way.

I asked God to show me if there was anyone that my heart wasn't right with; anyone with whom I needed to make peace in my own spirit. You know, that's really one prayer that the Lord likes to answer. Gently he began to put his thumb on certain areas of my heart. Hurts I have gained while pastoring, pain I have adopted while growing up and even issues I have had with God Himself about decisions that he has made in my life.

The thing about issues of the heart is that hurt is sometimes justified but it's never very helpful. In fact, hurt if left there to fester will only rob from you. It robs you of your joy and your peace while the person who wronged you has gone on with their life sometimes completely oblivious of your internal struggle.

I love what Jeremy has been saying as he has been preaching (ironically about the issues of the heart.) Sometimes the answer is so simple but it isn't always easy.

The answer to hurt and to pain towards someone in your life is to let it go. Simply to let it go. These last days as I had been preparing to get my physical heart reset, I have been resetting my spiritual heart. I was ready to let it all go. I was ready to take any hurt that I feel, wrap it up in a big giant grocery bag and hand it to the One who can handle the difficult issues of life; who can replace it with peace and joy.

You see there is something interesting about the heart. Most of the time, you don't notice it's beating. You don't even think about it as you are going about your daily business. That is, until there is something wrong. Then it becomes a big part of your life. It limits you. It worries you. You begin to make decisions around it. You begin to pull back just in case it starts acting up. You begin to put dreams on the shelf. It's the same way with the spiritual heart. You don't really notice it until something goes wrong. Then you feel the pain, the hurt, the debt, the jealousy, the pressure of wanting it to be the way it was. When you feel that pressure; that discomfort in your heart - there is something wrong and you have to deal with it.

Today, I went downstairs and danced to lovely worship music as I often do before I go to work.

This time something was different. This time, my heart did not go into palpitations - something that has happened everyday for a long time. When I was finished, I was so touched. This morning, I felt free.

Both my physical heart and my spiritual heart are in sync with the fresh steady beating of the Holy Spirit - of the One who created my heart.

Above all
Love
each other
deeply.
1 Pet. 4:8

Love

I debated on whether to go or not. I was tired because I had had a busy day the day before. But mostly because Sean wasn't feeling well. He was getting over a cold that hit him all of sudden and I just wasn't sure he would be in top form to be participating in a parade for Welcome Wagon. I talked to him and observed him and decided that we could do it. Once we got there, we realised that it was going to be much longer than we had anticipated, there was no access to a bathroom and guess what?! Of course, Sean needed to go. I looked at him. He looked tired. I thought about walking back to our car to go home but decided against it. He could sit in the wagon I was pulling if he wasn't feeling well for a while. That seemed to be a good idea to him as well.

We were one of the first to go. As we walked up a little incline and then down and up again, I booted Sean out of the wagon because I was getting tired already and we were going to be walking a fair bit. We were told that it was very slow but as we began walking, we soon realised that it really wasn't slow at all. When I told him he needed to walk, I also told him that I had a basket of candy and book marks and he was to feel free to go out into the crowd and pass them out at random - as much as he wanted. I wasn't sure he would.

Suddenly he grabbed a handful of candy and started weaving through the crowd handing it out. He ran back for book marks and started handing them to random people in the crowd, giving them to upraised hands just like a rock star. He kept running back to me, exclaiming, "This is awesome Mom. This is pleasing me so much. This is just pleasing me!" He ended up running way more than all of us who were walking in a straight line trying to move forward with our wagons and not look or feel like we were going to pass out in the heat. I looked at him as he moved in and out of crowds of people. He was smiling, his eyes were shining and I am sure for about an hour at least, he completely forgot how stuffed up he was and how much he just didn't feel up to it. He became alive doing something valuable.

My mind was brought back to a time years ago, when my heart was heavy about something personal I was going through. I felt pressed in my spirit and because of that, my whole body felt heavy. I felt like I was walking through molasses as I was walking through my day. I slowly walked to the photo centre in Costco, - my mind a trillion miles away. The lady that helped me asked how I was doing and I politely said, "Fine. And how are you?" glancing up at her as I asked her.

I never expected an answer. Never even wanted one - at least not a truthful one - especially since I hadn't given her a truthful one myself. I don't know why, but she thought I cared. And she started to cry. Right there in Costco, she started to cry. We moved aside to a corner and I looked her in the eyes, now really caring. I asked her what was wrong and she commenced to tell me that it was the anniversary of her daughter's death - a life cut far too short as she was just 20 when she died. I looked at her and my heart ached as I tried to imagine that kind of grief, watching a daughter waste away from a horrible disease. I told her I was sorry and that I would pray for her and then wiping away her tears, she had to go back to work and I went on my way.

Her story, however, wouldn't leave me. I thought about it for the next couple of hours so I went home and made a card and wrote in it that I would be thinking about her and praying for her and gave her my phone number. I walked back into Costco, to give it to her. When I got to where she was working, she had already gone home. Giving it to someone else to deliver it when she came back, I prayed silently that it would reach her at a time when she needed to read it (which I found out later that it did exactly that.)

Then I just went home.

But do you know what happened? I went home a lighter person. I went home with a spring in my step. I went home with love in my heart because I had helped someone. I had reached outside of my pain and helped someone who was going through something far more painful than I. It released me. It brought some healing. It refreshed me and filled me up. Suddenly, I saw some perspective.

That's what I saw in Sean that day. He reached outside of how he was feeling in order to bring happiness and lightness to someone else. In helping someone else, he helped himself more.

Suddenly I realised something. The Bible talks about the fact that His burden is easy and his yoke is light.

"Take My yoke upon you and learn from Me,
for I am gentle and humble in heart,
and YOU WILL FIND REST FOR YOUR SOULS.
For My yoke is easy and My burden is light."
Matthew 11:30

That verse has always been a mystery to me. Nothing about a burden or a yoke sounds easy or light. And today I think I am beginning to understand what it means. I think that his burden is love. That's what his burden is. If we are yoked or tethered to Him - He IS love!! So we will become that to those around us. His commission and life's purpose for us has always been love. Just love those around you. No judgements. No preconceived rules. No harsh assumptions. Simply love your neighbour as yourself - one of His highest commandments.

All the other things that we add to our lives that become a burden and a yoke to us are all added things - programs and busyness, when all he really wants us to do it reach out and love. All he really wants us to do is take on His mission - take on His call and love from wherever we are to wherever they are.

Love.

When we take on that burden and that yoke, something happens to us from the inside out and we find ourselves becoming free. We find ourselves healing. Suddenly we are not empty anymore. Suddenly, and I don't know how it happens, that the more we give out, the more we gain. When we are truly motivated by what God wants us to be motivated by, it releases us and frees us and fills us, taking us to heights we had never dreamed of.

So, today when I find myself exhausted and spread too thin, I am going to remember to take on his burden. Because I know what love does.

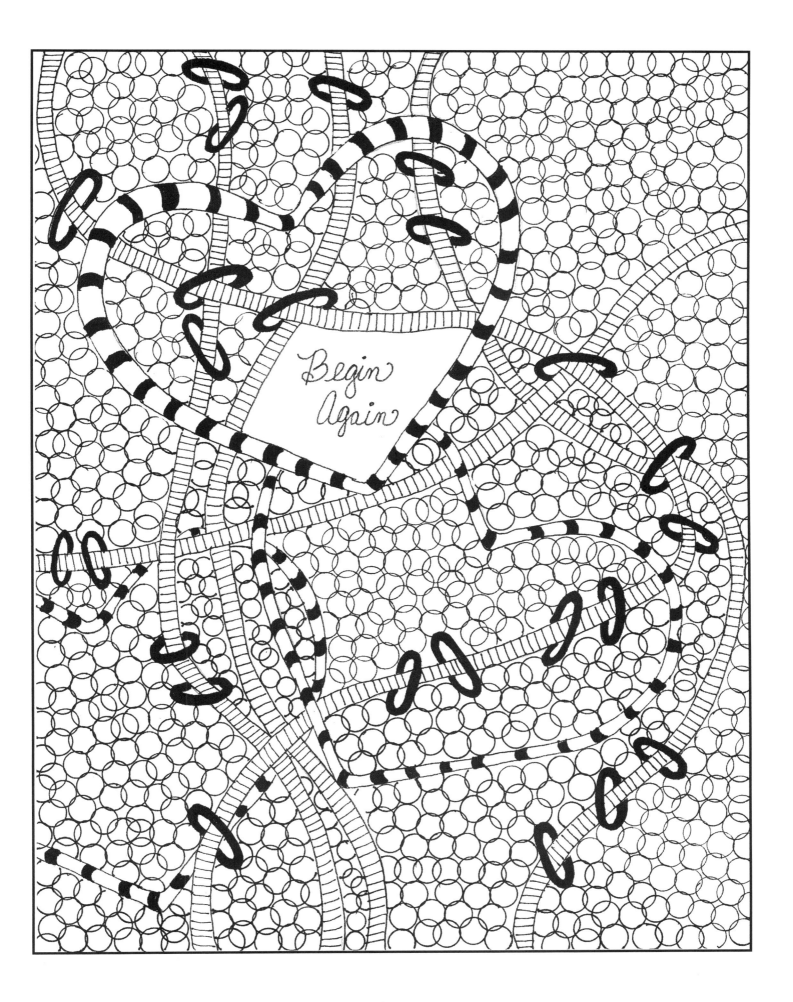

Heart Friends

Heart friends. That's what I call them. You know - those are the kind of friends that are easily connected to your heart. I have a few of them. I have a few of them here and a few of them scattered across the globe.

When my father in law was dying two and half years ago, we were visited by such friends; two of which were from England and we hadn't seen in years. To say that it was a treat would be an understatement of the year. It was not only touching that they came to support us, it was epic to see them; to spend time with them again.

Sitting around the table, eating meat and cheese with soft white buns, bright red strawberries with fresh homemade whipping cream, we realised that we had been friends for 3 decades. We hadn't talked in years, but it was as if we hadn't left each other; like we had just taken a long breath in order to start talking and sharing again. It was that magical.

We have created a thousand memories together, laughed until our bellies ached and cried buckets of tears.

Friendship is something money can't buy. It's something that you have to give yourself to - your heart, your journey. You have to be vulnerable - even raw at times. That's what we have shared with these guys. We have gone through moves, and babies, and deaths and weddings, and prodigals and everything in between, together.

Time is a beautiful thing for some friendships. Time tries and tests and weighs - how important; how deep you dug that well of friendship. and for these friendships, time proved that we dug the well deep. Rich, filled with power, redeeming, satisfying, loving, friendship.

How I love these people and how I love God for bringing them into our lives 30 years ago. That season we needed them so desperately.

When my oldest son heard that all six of us were getting together he said, "You know, Mom, things could get really silly." He remembered the laughter until the wee hours of the morning. We've talked about crazy things - silly inside jokes that make ONLY US laugh. We've talked about deep things - like faith and doubt, beauty and sorrow, lovely things and ugly things. We've shared meals, and vacations, and plays and missions trips and dinners and dozens of cheesecakes and saved the world a million times through our plans and thoughts. The list goes on and on.

This is what life is all about. Finding people who will become the words to the heart song you choose to sing; finding your people - your friends - who walk with you through the confusion, through the beauty, through the gross darkness and through the streams of light.

Time and distance has never separated our hearts and our lives from intertwining.

If you haven't found friendships like this, find them. If you don't have a tribe - or you don't have people around you as heart friends, look for them. Look long and hard. When you find them, invest in them. All of us need those surrounding us, linking arms with us and walking us through the messiness of life. Treat them like treasures - because they are. They won't be perfect because none of us are - but they will be vastly beautiful all the same.

You were called to be free. Serve one another humbly in love.

Gal. 5:13

On Loving Well

I used to see only black and white.

I was that person that got mad at you if you didn't treat me right going through the till. I was the one that let you know swiftly if my coffee wasn't hot enough. I was that person who honked at the cars that cut me off - not to let them know that I was there but to let them know that I was super angry at them. In my mind, you were either right or wrong. Lifestyles were either right or wrong. It was black and white and I left no room for colour or for grey.

I am not the opposite of who I was - I will still send my coffee back if it's too cold. I will still ask the teller if I am inconveniencing her if she acts like I have interrupted her day. I am rarely embarrassed or hesitant to state my true feelings. But these days, I am more often asking strangers if they want prayer; if they know that Jesus loves them or if they need anything. Now, I find myself looking beyond their outward actions and looking deep within their heart, knowing that there is a person who goes through pain just like me. There before me stands a person fighting for freedom in his/her life; struggling to stay above the water. I am realising more and more that people often carry heavy loads on their shoulders that they can't possibly lay down at the door of their work. Instead of a rebuke, they need an outstretched hand, they need a loving and kind word from a stranger. A snide remark will stick arrows in their back for a week, while a beautiful gesture of love might possibly change their life.

How interesting that Jesus actually came to earth to fulfil the law so that he could replace it with one word - love. That's not to say that he wanted us to run around killing each other in the name of freedom. He didn't take away boundaries or conscience. But he taught us that we need to follow a path that is so much greater and at the same time, much much harder. People that live in black and white think that love is a grand cop-out. Sure, just love people. But when you think about it, when you live by the principle of love, it's much harder than following a set of rules and the results so much better.

Jesus left us with two commands. Love God and love one another. When we live by the higher law we are freer. We have added colour to our lives.

Life is not a simple answer. Sometimes there aren't any easy solutions. In my years of ministry and counselling, I have learned that often there aren't hard and fast rules for a lot of things in this life. Often, it's hard to untangle the truth from the lie - the right from the wrong. There are so many variables. So instead of living in judgement, suddenly you realise that the better way is love. The noble gesture is a soft hand on a tired shoulder.

All of us need to be loved. All of us, no matter what age, race or religion need to feel important - we need to know that we matter deeply to the world around us.

I love the story in the Bible of the woman caught in adultery. The Pharisees brought the terrified woman before Jesus and told Him of her sin. Clutching stones in their hands, they were waiting for the signal from Jesus to stone her. It was simple to them. This woman was a sinner - she was caught. Stone her. What Jesus did next is a mystery to this day. As the crowd waited for his approval, silently He bent down in the dirt and began writing words on the ground. Then He looked up and simply said, "Okay, the person without any sin in their lives - YOU cast the first stone." No one could be that person because they all knew that they had sinned in their lifetime. He then turned to the panic stricken lady who was looking on with awe in her eyes. This is what he said, "Go and sin no more." How could he say that so casually? How could it be that easy for her to just go "and sin no more." Maybe she was in love with the man with whom she was committing adultery. Maybe it was an addiction to her. There are so many things that we don't know about this story.

This is how He was able to say it with such confidence; such conviction. Because instead of stones, she had experienced love. Instead of hate, she was bathed in kindness. Her very life was saved. And because her very life was saved with love, her soul was saved. She experienced the love of God and she was a different person.

Our love will change people.

When you go to the grocery store, look for people that need your love. Keep your eyes and heart open for those that need to hear a kind word or receive a smile.

Jesus didn't tell us to love people that believed the same as us. He didn't tell us to love in spite of... He didn't tell us to love even though...

He simply told us to love people. Simply love people no matter the race, no matter the religion, no matter the beliefs, and no matter the actions.

Love.

That's it.

Let's take a look at three ways to love well.

1. Don't keep score. Don't love only those people who can love you back. Don't just love people to show them you are great - you are lovely. Love them because they need to be loved, they want to be loved. Even if they can't love you back. Even if you love them in ways that are anonymous. Love them. Love someone for no reason. Love someone who you will never ever see again. Do it even if it doesn't make your name more popular; it doesn't bring anyone else into the church; it doesn't advertise ANYTHING at all - you are just showing genuine love to show love.

2. Love the way you want to be loved. What is your love language? On any given day, what would YOU want? What would make your day? Would it bless you if someone gave you a gift - just because...? Then choose someone to give a gift to. Would you love it if someone just came up to you and gave you a compliment; told you how much they appreciate you? Then do the same for someone. Would it make your day if someone left a card for Starbucks under your windshield? Then find someone who would love the same and do it for them. Do you know what that does? It heals you. It refreshes you. It uplifts you. Because love doesn't only help the one who receives it, it helps the one who gives it as well.

3. Give lavishly, wildly and generously out of your love bank today. I had a pastor once who said it was always good to error on the side of grace. I adopted that saying because I LOVE it. But I want to take that a step further and say that you can never error on the side of love. One of the things on my bucket list is to stand behind someone in the grocery store, step up and say, "I want to buy her groceries." I can't wait until one day I can do that.

I want to love with abandonment. I want to see my waitresses through eyes of love. I want to see my co-workers, my neighbours and those I meet, through eyes of love. I want to be motivated in my everyday life through eyes of love. Because I know that one day 2000 years ago, there was a Man who died for me. His motivation was sincere, genuine, lovely and wild love.

Tomorrow, when you wake up in the morning, choose to think this very question. "Who can I love today?" When you begin to wake up every morning with this thought, it will change your life.

I promise you.

This is the day that the Lord has made. Let us rejoice and be glad in it.

Butterflies

My nine year old son said it and it gripped me. I couldn't let it go.

He came home from school one day with a gift that he had made for Mother's Day. It was a really sweet gift - a small canvas painted orange because it is my favourite colour. On the canvas were several butterflies that were punched out from a hole punch. It was punched from paper that Sean had also painted. It was a beautiful piece of artwork that is now displayed proudly on my buffet table. It serves as a gift of love but also a constant reminder of what happened next.

He pointed to a butterfly that had blunt wings instead of pointed and rounded wings like all the others. He said sweetly, "Mom, I had to hide this from the teacher because if she would have seen it, she would have had me throw it away because it's not like the others. But Mom, I didn't want to throw it away because it's a rare butterfly. I knew you would see that too - and we don't throw away rare butterflies!" he exclaimed, his eyes shining proudly.

I looked at him. He got it. Life - in a nutshell - he got it. Don't throw away the butterfly because it doesn't look exactly like all the others.

He wasn't ashamed of it. He didn't hide the blunt wings under another butterfly. He didn't put it on the bottom out of the way. He put it right on the top in the centre! It was a treasured butterfly to him.

It reminded me of a workshop I went to one day. I came away from that evening with a thought from the main speaker that captured my heart. So many times we look at certain students and we wonder how we can fix them. In actuality we don't need to fix them at all.

We need to see the beauty, the uniqueness and the rarity of their beautiful souls. We need to grab ahold of their strengths and capitalise on them. Our goal isn't to change them, to make them look like all the other humans - like cookie cutter people. Our job is to spur them on into greatness. It's not about fixing them. It's completely about accepting them right where they are at. It's about seeing their strength and their uniqueness. It's not about clipping their wings so that they match the others. We don't need to match. We need to live our own story and let others live theirs. We need to let them be great in their own greatness and not measure greatness by our standard.

We were never meant to be a clone or a replica of the person next to us. We were meant to be deeply and completely ourselves - wildly and weirdly different and unique and messy and perfect in every way. We are all broken in some way or another - all of us show our brokenness in different ways. All of us are accepted by the Beloved - by Jesus. Jesus didn't tell us that he would love us when we healed ourselves. He told us that he would love us no matter what and it's in the love that the healing comes.

Those of us who work with people on a regular basis - let's not look at the ones with different wings and wonder how we can hide them or change them. Let our questions be different. Let's ask ourselves how we can love them where they are at, believe in them genuinely and help them to live and tell their story well. Let them have a voice. Let them see their importance in their world. We need their voice. We need their story and their magic.

I once heard someone say that they hated potential. I remember it clearly - I snickered and wholeheartedly agreed. I understand what he meant - that sometimes potential was another way of saying that they just weren't measuring up to what they could be doing in life. He was really talking about potential wasted. I got it then. But I don't agree anymore. I love potential. Because potential means greatness. Potential means hope. It is our job as caregivers, as nurturers, to tap into that potential. To lead them to the vast wide field of potential and let them see with their own eyes what they can do and what they can accomplish with their own voice; it's our job to give them hope. It's not our job to lead them to the "good little boy" next to them and ask them to be like him. The picture is so much bigger; so much wider than that.

Pastors, Teachers, Parents,
don't try to fix the butterflies that don't have wings like the others.
Don't try to change them.
Don't try to make them conform.
Do love them.
Do be proud of them.
Do see their beauty.
Please, please, please don't throw away
the butterfly with the straight wings.
We need it's beauty.

When you walk through the fire you will not be burned. The flames will not consume you.

Brokenness

Brokenness doesn't have to mean defeat. It doesn't have to mean failure.

We recently had to close our church down. Because it is so fresh in my mind , there are so many questions. There is a struggle that we did something wrong. When things like that happen, you keep replaying that season of life over and over again.

I am beginning to learn that God has another way of defining success. He doesn't promise that he will always bless what you are doing like you envision the blessing or that it will last forever or even that you will last forever. We have a hard time as Christians dealing with these issues. He told Moses to go to Pharaoh and tell him to let the Israelites go. Then he told them that he wasn't going to succeed. We always wonder why Moses didn't want to go - I am thinking that that was part of the reason.

In fact success and failure doesn't really matter to God in the sense that we as the world see it. What matters to Him is our heart. What matters to him is that we are following hard after his heart and his heart is love. We can love from the prison cell. We can love from the filthy alley way. We can love from the darkest loneliest of places.

I think that God defines success as being obedient. Coming to the table even when your heart is breaking. Simply showing up even when you don't feel like it.

Life is always a dance of learning when to let go and when to hang on. Sometimes it's harder to let go than it is to hang on to something you thought was going to turn out so differently. Yet, it takes maturity to see the difference.

Sometimes Jesus invites himself into your room of pain before he ushers you into his beautiful room of healing. We all want the healing before we experience the pain.

I am heart broken but I am not defeated. I feel torn but I am not destroyed.

You may be too. But there is good news.

We will find God in the dark places.
We will find God in the ugliness of this season.
We will find God in the ruins.

But you, O Lord, are a shield around me; you are my glory, the one who holds my head high. I cried out to the Lord, and he answered me. I lay down and slept, yet I woke up in safety, for the Lord was watching over me. I am not afraid of ten thousand enemies who surround me on every side. Victory comes from you, O Lord. May you bless your people.

God, Help Us Truly See

I don't know why I was cut to the core so deeply when I found out about Robin Williams death.

Maybe it was because I had been looking into anxiety and depression. Maybe it's because I myself have dipped my toe in waters of anxiety and depression. Or maybe it's because here was a man so loved, so entertaining, so successful in the worlds eyes, but even so, at the end of the day he felt the pain of death was sweeter than the pain of life. He was completely without hope. I was so sharply reminded that there are people all around us that are internally tortured and trying to live in their shattered worlds.

What can we do? Can we change the world? Can we turn the tide of the whole world to see hope and peace in the midst of struggles - in the midst of pain? Maybe not. But we can change our neighbours. We can change the people we work with, the people we pass by everyday. The people we go to Church with. We can change OUR world. In fact, we NEED to be changing our world.

It's time we give wings to our love. It's time we give feet to our message of grace and hands to our song of salvation.

The world and the Church need real. We need authenticity. The world needs us as broken and hurting people ourselves to reach out to the more broken and hurting.

We don't really need any more programs. We don't really need anymore fancy lights on our beautiful stages. What we need is to realise that there are people all around us dying - both on the outside and the inside. And they aren't just "out there." They are people literally around us - sitting in the pews next to us, staring into our eyes Sunday after Sunday.

Let's knock the walls of the church down and spill out into the world, out in the community, out into their hearts. Because we live in a broken and pained world today that needs hope, that needs peace, that needs a glass of water. We need to reach out and feed a starving child.; clothe a homeless man.

It's all about them. That's all Jesus asks of us - that we see them. We don't make it about ourselves, and our programs. We don't make it about our hurt feelings, our insecurities, our betrayals, and our questions with no answers. But that we make it out about them - the world and those around us. Jesus was always reaching out - his whole life about the people around Him - always them.

We need to look at the people we see everyday. Really look at them.. Look beyond their blue and brown eyes and into their souls. We need to look beyond the beautiful body and see the broken pieces within. We need to hear behind the smooth words and listen to their screams and cries for help.

Somehow in this world of beauty, in this world of technology and fakeness, our senses have been dulled. Jesus looked beyond the paralytic, he looked beyond the man that couldn't move and said that his sins were forgiven him. Why? Because he saw a man crying out for salvation and for freedom of the soul even more than he was crying out for movement. He looked beyond the physical needs of the woman at the well and saw that she was woman through and through who just wanted to be loved, who just wanted to be valued like everyone else. He saw. He truly saw.

God, help us. God help us to truly see.

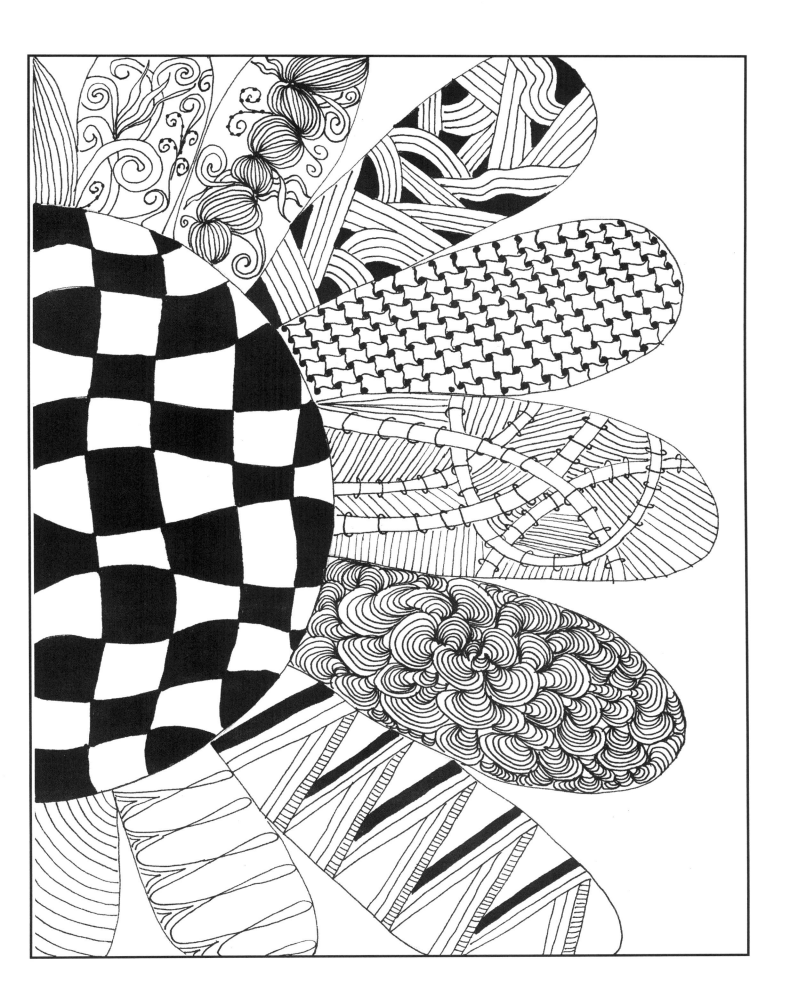

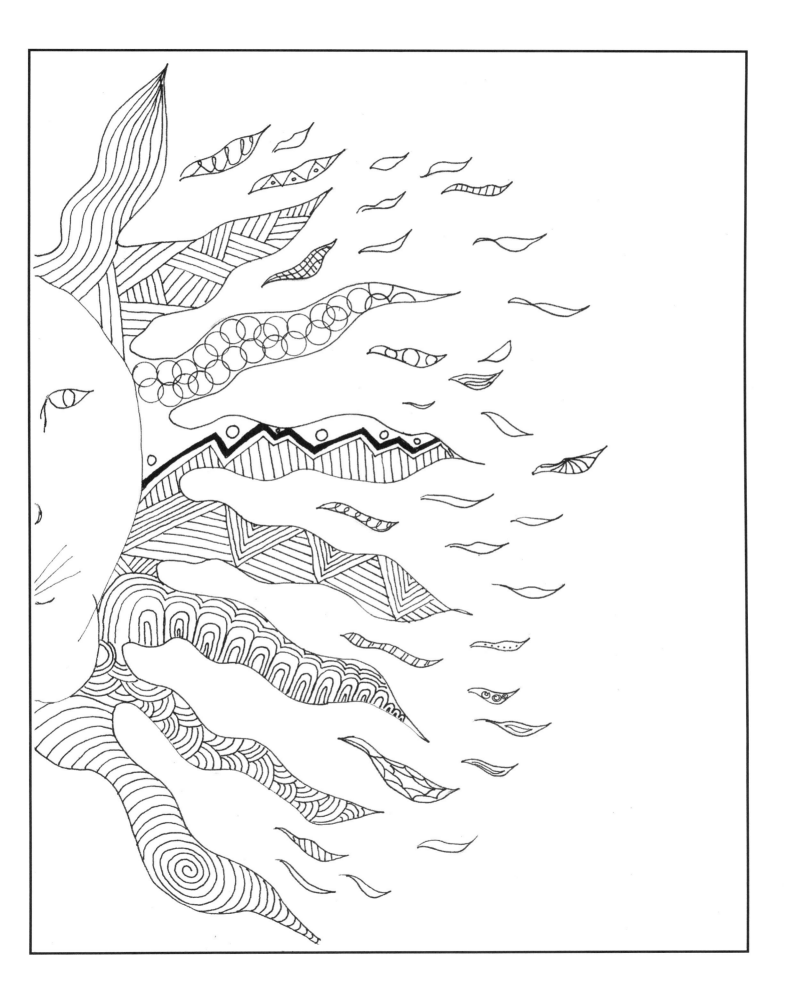

Words Matter

Several months ago a friend of mine sent me a picture of a little note I had written to her when she lived in my town. Immediately I smiled. I remember when I slipped it in her Bible. She had left her Bible at my place so before I gave it back to her, I slipped a few notes randomly throughout her bible.. Suddenly my mind wandered to all those words I have written to people. There are literally people all over the world that bare my words on their heart. You see, I decided a long time ago that I wanted my words to carry life. I wanted my words to carry healing. As adults, I want people to remember a woman in their childhood - I want them to remember a woman with a flowing, crazy sparkling dress and bling in her hair that bent down to their level and whispered gently in their ear, "You can" when they lived in a world of "you can'ts."

Do you remember those people in your lifetime? Do you remember those people who believed in you; who encouraged you to not give up and to dreams big dreams? I have those people in my life. I remember one such lady in my 8th grade. She was my English teacher. I can't even remember her name. I loved that woman. I was going through a difficult time in my life at that time. She picked up on it. I don't remember why. I don't remember if my grades were slipping or if I shared something in my journal writing or what. But she had me stay after class so that she could talk to me. Really she just listened. She just listened to me tell her everything in my life that was upside down right at that moment. She listened and she encouraged me. She encouraged me to write. She encouraged me to dream. She told me that I would be okay. I won't ever forget that. I have never told her how or what that meant to me. She may never know. But she touched a chord in my heart. She made a difference in my life. I want to be her - I want to be my English teacher to other people around me.

I've thought of people in the states, in Japan, in Canada, in the Philippines, in Thailand, in Africa - that I have spoken words of encouragement to; words of hope. How many of them still have those pieces of paper, those text messages, those cards, those emails? How many still remember?

We have to remember that our words hold life or death in them. We have to remember the power of those words. Because what my friend didn't know is that the exact time when she sent that picture to me, I was asking God if I had made a big enough impact; if I had been enough, if there were enough people changed and healed and loved through my actions and through my words. She didn't know how much that one text message impacted me.

This is gold. This is what the Christian life is all about. This is what community is all about. Life giving words. I believe that this is what Jesus meant when he said, "Your faith has made you whole." He was encouraging - he was saying "good for you." He was patting them on the back for a job well done.

I want to leave in the wake of my life, people impacted by my words - whether or not I ever knew it. At the end of the day, I want a line-up of people clutching little pieces of paper; holding text messages, remembering words spoken like gold; like treasures.

In this crazy mixed up world that we live in, everyone needs to be loved; everyone needs to dream; everyone needs to believe that they are worth it. I want to be that voice; I want to be that whisper into their soul:

> You can do it.
> You are worth it.
> You are loved.

Who do you need to encourage this week? Who do you need to speak words of life to? Close your eyes. Ask God - he will tell you.

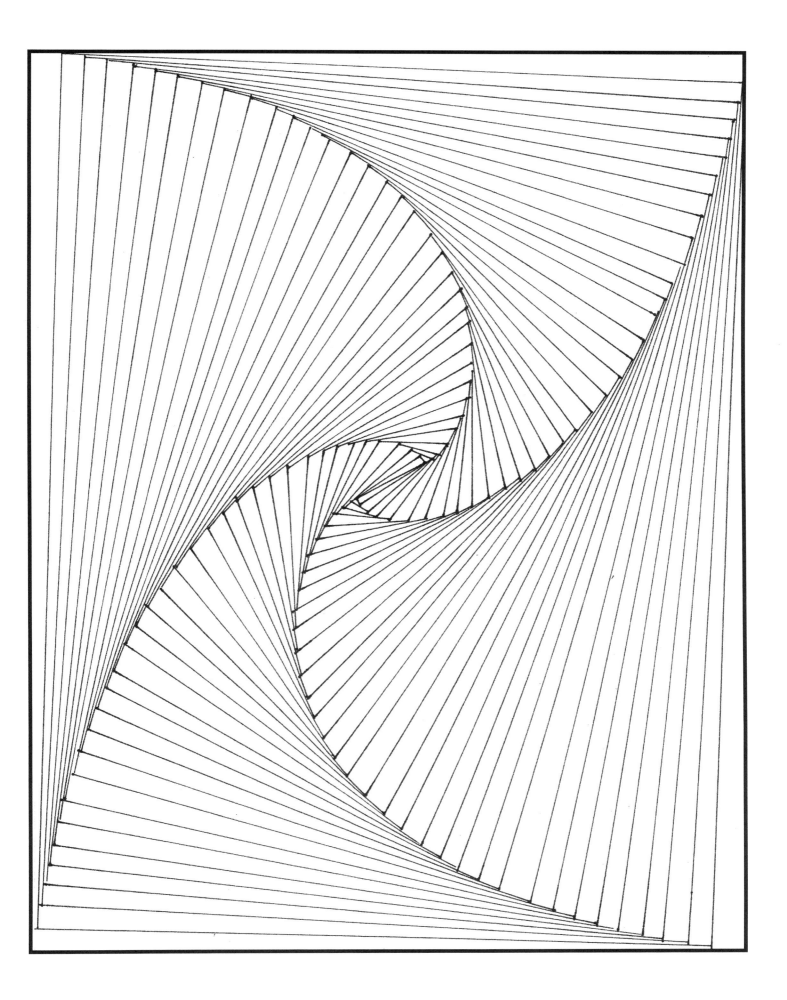

Be completely humble and gentle;
be patient, bearing with one another
in love.

Her Face

Her face still haunts me. I still feel the searing pain in my heart when I think of her. I was in the parking lot ready to start my engine when she started hobbling toward me. She was crippled and stared at me with one eye. The other one was completely gone. She tried to reach me, to talk to me but before she could, I sped away. I was busy. I had a million things to do that day; appointments to make. As soon as I sped away, I felt my stomach churn with guilt. Why did I leave her standing there? I knew that she needed money or something. I knew she was a beggar. I felt a sense of panic when she walked over to me; she unsettled me in my perfect little world.

I literally felt like the Pharisee in the Bible who was too busy to stop and help the man on the side of the road who was bleeding and dying. What message did I give? What life did I want to lead? I want to lead a life of kindness, of generosity, of love and yet I was driving away from the very woman who needed me most that very moment. Did that make me a hypocrite?

The guilt didn't leave even as my adult son assured me that I had done the right thing; that I didn't need to give to everyone who asked for money or for favours. But she really did need me. She really did need money. It wasn't like she could go out and get a job or something. It wasn't like she was lazy. I had seen her cart. She had a few meagre belongings inside of her cart.

Some time later, I found myself marching back out to the car with a mission in mind. I drove to the parking lot to find the woman; to offer her food or a prayer or a listening ear. Sadly, she wasn't there. I never forgot her face. I never forgot her deformed body slowly making her way to my car; for some kindness; for some peace in a stormy life; a cool ointment on a seeping wound. I wasn't that for her.

Did she have family? Was she lonely? Did she need someone to care; to listen to her; to love her? Everyone deserves to be loved. Everyone deserves to know that they are valued; they are important and they are special. Did she know that? In the depths of her spirit, did she know that she mattered every bit as much as I matter?

I held a little girl one day as she clung to me and cried.   Her sobs wracked her tiny little body but she never told me what was wrong. She never used her words and she never felt comfortable doing so. What sorrow did she hold in that sweet little body of hers. What pain locked her heart and bound her so that she wouldn't share it with anyone else.   I wanted to help; to show her I cared and I did. I sat there as she cried. I sat there and hugged her as tight as I could without hurting her - willing her to feel better; willing her to feel just a little bit of joy. I knew that she had gone through so much in her short little life; she had seen things that she should have never seen; felt things that she should have never felt; heard things that should have never reached her ears.

Life can be cruel. Life can be hard. Life can be impossible.

If I could find that woman in the parking lot today, what would I tell her? If I could give that little girl I hugged a message, what message would I give her?

I would tell them that they are treasures.

I would tell them that there is hope. While there is still life, there is still hope. And even in death there is hope, because there is Heaven.

I would tell them that one day it will get better. That they won't always be in this storm.   That there is greatness somehow, somewhere for them.

I would tell them that they matter.

I would tell them that they are loved; maybe not by everyone that they wanted to be loved by but they are loved by Jesus.

I think that we should be generous. Generosity doesn't always mean giving money to someone. We can be generous with our time, our words, our kindness. I think that we are not supposed to be wrapped up in our own thoughts, our own agenda, our own lives as much as we are some days.

When Jesus walked this earth, he was generous with his time. He was not only generous to those whom he loved. He was generous to Peter and John whom he loved but he didn't stop there. He was generous to Zacchaeus who climbed up into a tree because no one would let him push through the crowd to see him - but he was not a well liked man. He was a criminal and certainly not generous with anyone - still Jesus chose to reach out to him. He reached out to everyone around him - even Judas who betrayed him and ultimately killed his physical body. Still he gave to him - still he chose to share his life, his words and his food.

I am learning to look around me everyday.
Who can I be generous to?
Who can you be generous to today?

Kisses in the Wind

It was a domino effect. I was late waking up, I was late getting Dylan to the bus stop and then I was late getting Sean to school. I knew that that would make me late for my next two appointments.

When I dropped him off at school he got out slowly and sauntered towards the school door. He wasn't depressed or trying to be slow, he was just enjoying life as he walked. When he got there he turned and waved at me. I waved back. He waved again and held the door open for two kids scurrying to class. He stood there in the doorway and blew a kiss at me. I blew one back and then put my car in reverse. He blew another kiss so excited by this game, I blew one back and started to back the car out. Once more, he blew a kiss and I turned. Out of the corner of my eye, I saw his face fall that I didn't return the kiss. He was late and I was late. I started to drive away with a twinge of guilt. I looked back to where he had been standing and he was gone. A stronger twinge of guilt. And then panic swept in, a big massive wave of panic. What if that was the last I ever saw him? What if something happened today at school and the last time I ever saw him, I was backing out, denying him that one last kiss? Would I ever be able to live with myself? I knew that I couldn't.

Tears started swimming in my eyes. Clutching the steering wheel, crying, I circled the school with an internal struggle inside of me. Should I park the car and cancel all my appointments today - make sure everything is okay in the school? One should never give in to panic of every day life. But one should always give in to the leading of the Holy Spirit. But which was this? Life always seems to be a dance of " did He say… or am I just thinking..." I decided that it was the latter because of how it caught my emotions. If it's God it usually catches my spirit, but not my emotions so deeply.

I started to proceed to my appointments for the day but my mind was still on that moment. Sean knew that he had school to go to and he loves school and he loves his teacher. But he knew what he wanted in the moment and that was to blow kisses to me. He chose to be present instead of hurried. He was in his own little "not rushed and peaceful" world. In his mind, he has school all day every day for 12 years. Today, school could wait just a little bit while he blew kisses in the wind at me. I applaud that.

When I was a young teenager, there was a lady that attended our church. I really looked up to her. I aspired to be like her. She was always busy, always in a hurry, always running late. When she came to the door to pick something up, she would be insanely rushed - massive, thick ,curly hair blowing in the wind as she whisked out to the car finishing up her story as she ran to her next appointment.

She seemed to have several balls up in the air and was desperately harried and busy and loving life. I pictured my life like that years from that point. I pictured a baby in tow with little kids at my feet, talking on the phone while I was baking cookies. I pictured talking on the phone to person after person giving them advice and comfort and prayers while I was making supper and vacuuming the floor getting ready for company that night. I romanticised that busy life. It's exactly what I aspired to do and when I got married that is exactly what I did. Being in the ministry all of our married life, juggling ministry, home life, and work life and volunteer life and friendships, that's exactly what my life looked life for long seasons.

But I am writing a new story. And in that new story, I am not so rushed. I won't make back to back counselling appointments in the evening like I did for so many years. And I won't make that calendar so full that I forget to be in the moment. I am beginning to learn not to jump every time I get a text message or notification on my iPhone for Instagram or Twitter or Facebook, those things can wait. They can wait. While I enjoy the moment.

I understand that there are jobs, there is reality. There is the clock and all those things are important. But what I am advocating is to rethink our lives a bit. Sometimes what we thought was so important aren't really the important things at all. Sometimes the things that we thought weren't that important are really the most important things in our lives.

It seems like in today's society, or at least in my mind, that the more demands you have, the more people calling, texting, writing you, the more things you have to do or go to or speak at or be in charge of, the more you are IN demand - the more loved you are; the more valuable you are; the more important you are. My new story says that

I am important even if my phone never rings, I am important even if I never come to anyone's rescue today, even if I didn't save anyone's life. Even if I didn't run myself ragged by running here and there trying to get way too much accomplished in a day, I am valuable, I am loved, and I am so important.

Yes I am writing a new story. And in my new story, I have time to blow kisses in the wind to my son.

Come to me, all you who are weary and burdened, and I will give you rest. Matthew 11:28

You are to shine
so brightly
that you reflect
the beautiful
Colours
of His precious
grace and love.

Matt. 5:15

Let There Be Light

In Genesis it says that God looked out over the vast darkness and void of the earth and said,
"Let there be light."
And there was.

Simply, with one sentence, with one command from the creator of the universe - light was created. Day was made. Not only is this impossible to do - create light out of a command of your voice, it was also pretty amazing because light had not even existed up until then.

Imagine a world of total and complete darkness - Completely void - a black hole in the universe .

Light hadn't been "invented" yet. The world knew no light. God out of his creativity thought up this great thing we call light, and day. The magnificent, dazzling ball of fire we call the sun. He dreamed it and he created it.

One day many years ago, I was going through one of the darkest days of my life. I felt completely bound up in a hopeless situation - one in which I couldn't find an answer; a solution. I was literally stuck in a bubble of darkness while the world went on with their lives.

As I was reading the Bible I saw this Scripture and it was as though God dropped the verse right into my heart. It jarred me - like a pebble being dropped in the bottom of a glass vase.

I knew that God needed to breathe his light in my dark world.

That's exactly what he did. It wasn't immediate. Sometimes God's breakthroughs are immediate and sometimes it is a process. The point is, to reach out to the One who can make light out of nothing; make the sun out of a big void.

Are you going through a dark time? Are you going through a time of so many questions and no answers? Let the God of the universe breathe his eternal light into your gross darkness.

I promise you, He will. No matter what you are going through, no matter who you are, He has the Light for your dark world.

I have seen it first hand.

Summer & Hollyhocks

This summer I could see it from my kitchen window. Every morning when I turned on my dearly loved Keurig coffee machine, I looked out the window and I smiled.

It was my tallest Hollyhock. Hollyhocks are one of my favourite flowers. I think that they are so romantic and free flowing and strong and beautiful. They are kind of artsy and I love artsy things.

But this particular Hollyhock - well this one taught me something.

It taught me that in the midst of hail, hurricane force winds and cold, cold spurts when it was supposed to be hot - I can stand strong; I can stand tall and I can be beautiful.

I remember after the third hailstorm this summer - looking outside at my flowers. It looked like a marigold massacre. Bit and pieces of petals and leaves and stems strewn all over my garden; vegetables had totally given up and pansies were one dimensional - they looked like a cruel painting against my steps. It was awful weather for any plant to survive.

Then a day or two later, I noticed something. My Hollyhocks - even though they were horizontal - they were blooming. They had been flattened; trampled by the weather, but still they found the strength to bring forth this beautiful bloom from their gangly stalks.

And then a few days later I looked and gasped. There was my tallest one -standing upright. Not laying on the ground anymore. It was taller than I was. It was beautiful and extravagant and strong. You would have never guessed in a million years what storms that Hollyhock had to weather. In amongst the weeds, the less than perfect soil, the terrible weather, it chose to be outrageously lovely.

It felt like it was cheering me on every day. "Yeah, Faith, you can do it! It doesn't matter if you've had an achingly cold and harsh summer; it doesn't matter if the storms keeps coming - you can do it I I've done it so can you!"

The bible talks about being more than a conqueror. I preached on that a few months ago. I have come to believe that being more than a conqueror has a lot more to do with your resolve to serve Jesus in the midst of "it all" rather than having all the circumstances line up perfectly for your enjoyment. I think that being more than a conqueror means that you weather the storms of life knowing that you won't run away from the one who calls you his son or daughter. You may have questions - you may be confused ;and you may even be a little bit angry - but you know Jesus enough. You have forged that relationship enough. You have dug the wells of friendship with Jesus in a deep way. You have enough history with Him to know that he is still God, he is still good and he can still be deeply trusted and loved with abandonment. That's what I believe being more than a conqueror is.

So this particular summer I found myself looking out my kitchen window, first thing in the morning - for my Hollyhock to greet me. Yes, I can do it - through the storms, through the ugliness and the upside down seasons, through the mixed up and crazy turns of life; through the cruel and really really hard parts.

I can do it, I know I can.

Our Journey

Therefore, since we are surrounded by such a great cloud of witnesses,
let us throw off everything that hinders and the sin that so easily entangles.
And let us run with perseverance the race marked out for us,
Hebrews 12:1

When I see this verse, I usually think of those people that have gone on before - cheering us on. My son, my grandmother and grandfather and now my father in law. I picture them cheering me on, telling me that I can make it; I can do it. It's a comfort and a joy even though I really don't understand all of the implications of heaven and those that are waiting for me.

One particular morning when I read this, one word literally jumped out at me - no it screamed at me. One little TWO LETTER word.

US. "Let us run the race marked out for US." What does this mean? This means that we wake up in the morning and we ask ourselves "What are we supposed to do today? Where are we supposed to be in our journey? What challenges do we give ourselves? What people do we reach out to? What amazing things are we going to do?"

I think that this life especially in North America offers so many distractions to deter us from our journey and cause us to find our feet on that of another journey besides our own. These are only a few examples.

Jealousy.
Anger.
Intimidation.
Comparison.
Fear.
People pleasing.
Entertainment

When our minds are cloudy with any of these things that I mentioned we rob ourselves of time. It becomes hard to find out what our own personal journey even is - let alone WALK on it. We don't leave any room to write our own story.

God has literally given us a path and he says, "Walk". That means we don't have time to wonder why Timmy can afford a big screen TV and we can't. Or why we can't get a job when we are looking and others aren't. It even means that we can't sit and worry about our daughters, our sons, our mothers, fathers and neighbours and try to manipulate their lives into working better.   Our distractions aren't always self serving or evil. Often our distractions come packaged as a very serving, loving, caring individual.

When caring for another individual robs us of our own journey, we have jumped onto another path. We have forgotten ourselves and our mission.

Let's not put our story, our book, on the shelf in leu of living any kind of life that is not our own.

It's time to put the "what if's" down.
It's time to put the "Maybe I should have's" down.

It's time to look down at our feet and see the race that God has set before us. Let's take those steps, however hard, however easy they are - because this is OUR journey. Let us own our journey.

Let's begin to write our story.

You will never live today again. You will never live this moment again. So spend it wisely.

Follow Your Heart

I have been asked how I do my doodles. I giggle inwardly every time someone asks me because I remember the first time I asked my friend how she did it. Her answer was always "Just follow you heart." It frustrated me a little bit because I wanted hard and fast rules. Now, when someone asks how I doodle, I want to say, "Just follow your heart." Because now that I do a lot of doodling, I understand.

I think the key for me is to have a pattern of lines or shapes or whatever and repeat it. Often, I look over my drawings and add more and then look again and even add more. It makes such a full and rich page when you add. It also depends on how busy you want your page to look. You can fill every available white spot on the page or you can leave large spaces of white.

It's important to note that there is absolutely no right or wrong way to doodle. This is your art and art is very ambiguous and often hard for the person who likes hard and fast rules.

I find my greatest doodles are when I just let go and do what I love. Maybe I will end up loving that doodle - maybe I won't. The point to doodling really is to give wings to your freedom - to your art. That's why there aren't any hard and fast rules to doing it.

Sometimes when I sit down with a blank piece of paper, I have a thought in mind of what I would like it to look like. Sometimes I have absolutely no idea and I just start making lines - the first thing that comes to my head. Then it grows and I get other ideas and fresh thoughts.

Often, I trace a part of the doodle just to see if I like it. Sometimes I trace nothing because it is flowing better.

Also, I have doodled a piece of art and then looked at it and thought "I don't like this." Then later when I looked at it, realised that it just needed one thing and it became one of my favourites. I have included one such drawing in this book, actually. Don't ever completely discount something you have created until you take a look at it later after you have given yourself some distance.

As with any art, the more you practice it, the more confidence you gain and the more you see your own style and what stance you want to take on with that particular medium of art.

I have included a couple of instructions on how particular lines are done. You will find lots of great ideas on the internet too. I have found a treasure trove of ideas and they grow from there into your own works of art with your own additions.

After the instructions are practice pages. I have also included a page that I have partially done. You can leave it as it is. You can add whatever you would like to the crazy squares or you can add to the squares and the circles. Do you whatever you want - it's for you to have fun with.

I hope this inspires you to start your own art. If you do, please share it with me. I would love it see it!!

Happy doodling!!

Happy Doodles

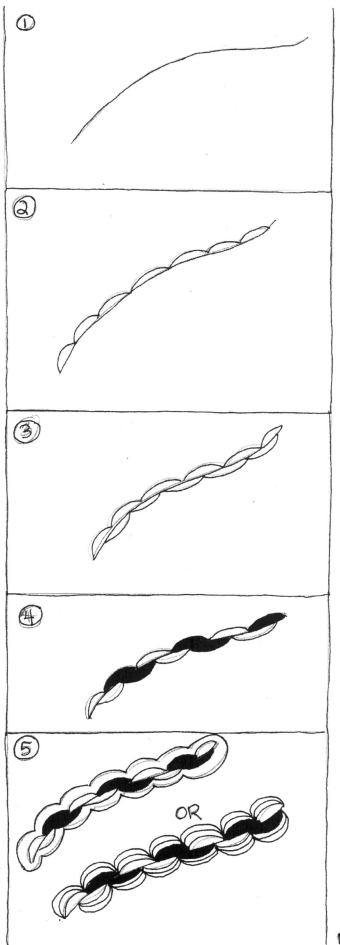

Add Embellish-
ments of any
Kind,

①

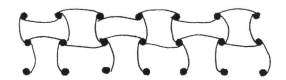

②

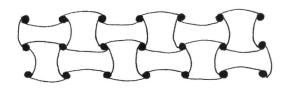

③ You can stop here or:

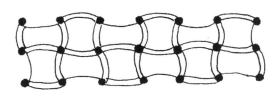

④ You can add outlines

⑤ You can further add lines, shapes or shading.

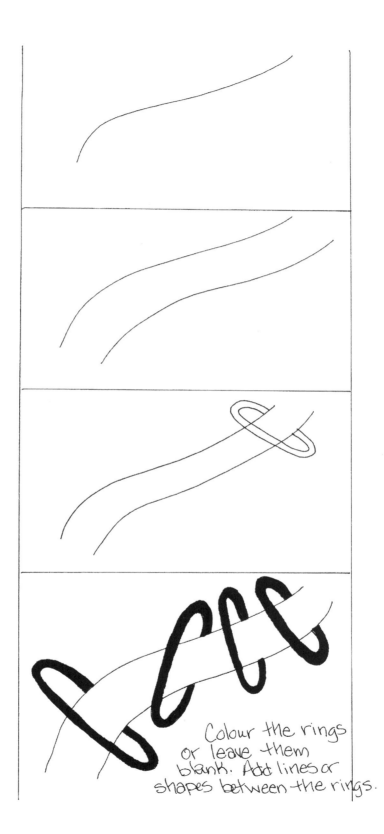

Colour the rings
or leave them
blank. Add lines or
shapes between the rings.

Bookmarks & Cards

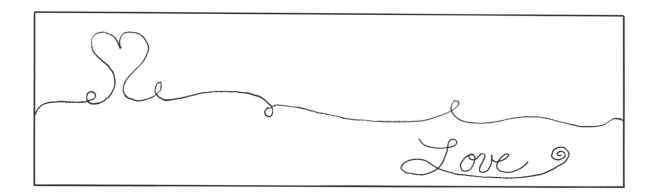

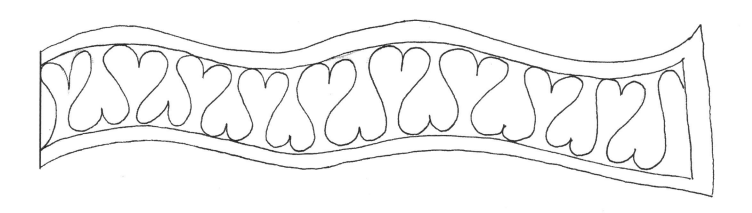

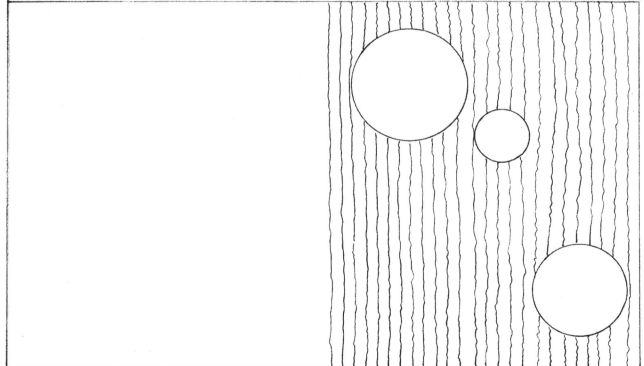

About Faith

Faith Hazell has a passion for people. Her desire is to love as Jesus loved - to make an impact on the world around her.

Born and raised in Japan, she learned what it was like to live on little and appreciate much. At a young age she learned that God uses mysterious ways and beautiful people to provide food and finances. Her heart is to always be that person for others.

As an adult, she has been in the ministry for 30 years, serving as youth group leader, various leadership roles, traveling minister, assisting a missions school and pastoring with her husband.

She has a family of four children living on earth, one in heaven, five grandchildren, (and one on the way). Her family brings her joy and comfort as she sees Gods hand at work in their lives every day.

She currently works at a kindergarten/preschool, lovingly teaching the children entrusted to her - a job in which she has found total fulfilment.

Her blog, *"Through Eyes Of Faith"* and artwork have been an inspiration to many. You can catch up on her writings at faithhazell.blogspot.ca.

Made in the USA
Charleston, SC
25 April 2016